Contents

Series Title 3
Discipline: Accounting 3
Equity Explained 4
    Sole Trader 5
    Partnership 5
    Companies 6
Introduction to Statement in Changes in Equity 8
The Link 9
Sole Trader Examples 10
Introductory Tasks ~ Sole Trader 11
    Task #1 12
    Task #2 12
    Task #3 12
Solutions ~ Sole Trader Tasks 13
    Solution ~ Task #1 13
    Solution ~ Task #2 13
    Solution ~ Task #3 13
Partnerships Examples 14
Partnership Tasks ~ Capital Account only 16
    Task #1 16
    Task #2 16
    Task #3 16
Solutions ~ Partnership Tasks (Capital Account only) 17
    Solution ~ Task #1 17
    Solution ~ Task #2 17
    Solution ~ Task #3 18
Partnership ~ Capital and Current Accounts 18
    Worked Task 19
Partnership Tasks ~ Capital and Current Accounts 20
    Task #1 21
    Task #2 21
Solutions ~ Partnership Tasks (Capital and Current) 22
    Solution ~ Task #1 22
    Solution ~ Task #2 23

Company Examples	24
Wellie Limited	24
Layouts	25
Company Worked Task	26
Further Worked Example	26
Further Examples	27
Beeswax Limited	27
Albatross Limited	27
Company Tasks # 1 – 6	28
Task #1 ~ Eastern Traders Ltd	28
Task #2 ~ Sunfield Industries Ltd	28
Task #3 ~ Mac Merrin Ltd	29
Task #4 ~ Ratu Limited	29
Task #5 ~ Harlequin Products Ltd	30
Task 6 ~ Palladian Pottery Limited	30
Solutions ~ Company Tasks #1 – 5	31
Solution ~ Eastern Traders	31
Solution ~ Sunfield Industries Ltd	32
Solution ~ Mac Merrin Limited	33
Solution ~ Ratu Limited	34
Solution ~ Harlequin Products Ltd	35
Solution ~ Palladian Pottery	36
Worksheet Method for a Company	37
Washdyke Tilers Limited	37
Solution ~ Washdyke Tilers Limited	39
Author Background	40

Series Title

Discipline: Accounting

Topic: Statement of Changes in Equity

- Want to get straight to the topic?
- Want material 'lesson ready' or 'student ready'?
- Teach a Topic does just that.
- This book covers the Statement of Changes in Equity and follows this format:
- What is Equity?
- Equity explained for:

    - Sole Trader
    - Partnerships
    - Companies

- Layouts for each type of business and worked tasks for:

    - Sole Trader
    - Partnerships
    - Companies

- Practise tasks for each business type.
- Solutions to practise tasks.
- Detailed explanation of terms, how solutions were arrived at, how to use a worksheet as a cross-check for layouts.

All that you need for a two or three hour lesson or for a thorough understanding on this topic.

Equity Explained

Equity is
"... the residual interest in the assets of the entity after deduction of its liabilities".

Equity is the amount of money (capital) that is invested in a business. It is shown in the Proprietorship (Owner's Equity or Capital) part of the Balance Sheet.

This can be defined as the owner's interest or the proprietorship in the business. This is the amount left over after all of the business's liabilities have been paid. That is, it is the amount the owner has invested in the business.

The term "equity" may be replaced by "owner's equity" or "proprietorship" (in the case of sole traders and partnerships) or "shareholders funds" (in the case of a company). Whichever term is used, it points to the same thing: the difference between assets and liabilities.

There are two aspects to the concept of owner's equity:
- introduced equity
- internally generated equity

Introduced Equity – is the capital the owner puts into the business. This can be in the form of cash contributions, or it can be physical assets such as land, buildings, vehicles etc; or intangible assets such as patents, copyrights etc. Thus, it is the value contributed by the owner to establish or expand the business.

Withdrawals ie drawings are the opposite of contributions. They reduce the capital of the business. If it is goods/stock that has been used by the owner it still has a monetary value.

Decreases in liabilities will increase the value of the equity.

- **Internally Generated Equity** – in simple terms, this is the profit of the business that is retained in the business. Profit is the difference between the revenues earned by the business and the expenses incurred in generating those revenues. Net profit (or loss) is brought in from the Income Statement.

There are two things that can be done with profit:
- retaining it within the business
- distributing it to those who are entitled to it – ie the owners

Components of Owner's Equity
Although the concept of owner's equity is the same for:
- sole traders
- partnerships
- companies
  - there are differences in the terms used to identify the items that make up the capital of a business.

Sole Trader

Owner's Equity
   capital invested
   plus net profit (or less net loss)
   less drawings

- drawings are usually cash, but may also be goods taken from the business for private use
- drawings are recorded as a reduction in both the owner's equity account and an asset (either bank or inventory)

An extract from the Proprietorship section of the Balance Sheet:

	$	$
Proprietorship		
Capital 1 April 2017	65,000	
Additional Capital	8,000	
	73,000	
Net Profit	123,000	
	196,000	
Less Drawings	89,000	
Capital 31 March 2018		107,000

Partnership

Similar to the owner's equity section for a sole trader. Each partner has a separate capital account, and a separate drawings account. Any transactions made by a particular partner that affect the amount of capital contributed to the partnership are recorded in these accounts for that particular partner.

At the end of each accounting period, when the profit (or loss) is calculated, each partner's current account is allocated with the share of the net profit (or loss) as set out in the partnership agreement.

If a partner makes an advance to the business as a loan, this must be kept separate from the capital accounts of the business. Likewise, if a partner borrows from the business. Any interest payable will also be treated separately from drawings and profit.

The current account is where all the shares of profits, losses and drawings are recorded.

	$	$	$
Proprietorship			
Capital 31 March 2017			
D Clark	100,000		
B Brown	90,000	190,000	
Current Account 31 March 2017			
D Clark	25,000		
B Brown	12,000	37,000	227,000

Companies

Here the owner's equity (or shareholders' equity) as it is commonly called) is separated into two main categories or sources of capital, which are:

	$	$
Shareholders' Funds 31 March 2017		
Authorised Capital – 100 000 shares @ $1 each	100,000	

- share capital – which represents the amount of assets invested in the company by the shareholders (in a public company this is the amount paid for the shares
- retained earnings (or accumulated losses), which reflect the monies earned (or lost) by the company and retained in the business

Share Capital

The amount invested in the company by the shareholders is called paid up capital. The share is the smallest part that the company's capital is divided into. A share entitles the holder to receive a proportionate part of the profits distributed by the company and to take part in the affairs of the company to the extent provided by the articles of association.

There are various types of share:
- ordinary
- preference
- particpating preference
  - which confer different rights on the shareholder.

You will also see the terms authorised capital and issued capital in most public company balance sheets.

Authorised Capital

This is the amount and number of shares the company is authorised by its memorandum of association to issue. Most companies have more authorised capital than issued capital.

Issued Capital

This is the amount and number of shares actually issued. If the full amount has been paid for each of these shares, the issued and paid up capital will be the same. However, occasionally shares have partly paid, as there are instalments to be made.

Retained Earnings

In a sole trader and partnership the total profit goes to the owners but a company does not have to distribute or pay out all of its profits each year. The amount withheld, is held as a revenue reserve and is called Retained Earnings.

Reserve Accounts

Companies may also have Capital Reserves – these represent gains that are not generally part of the operations of the business. Examples are:
- gains from revaluation of land
- fluctuations in currency valuation

These reflect the amount of profits (after tax) earned by the company and retained in the business. This is a reserve account. Profits that are not retained ie profit paid out to shareholders as dividends, are the company equivalent of the sole trader and partnership drawings accounts.

Share Premium Reserve

This account arises when shares are issued for more than their par (or face) value. For example, if shares having a face value of $1 are issued for $1.50 each, the extra 50 cents collected by company from the issue is placed in this account. Note: we are referring to an issue of new shares by the company. The buying and selling of shares on the stock exchange has no effect on the capital or share premium reserve of the company.

Asset Revaluation Reserve

This account arises when assets, such as land and buildings, are revalued to their current values. Obviously, only major assets that are likely to increase in value over time will have an effect on this account. Note, however, that if these assets subsequently lose value, the reduction should also be recorded in this account. Note also that it is an **unrealised gain (or loss)**.

Example:
```
    dr    Land                                   700,000
          cr    Asset revaluation reserve              700,000
```

The land is debited with the additional value the asset revaluation reserve receives the credit. No cash is involved.

A revaluation reserve falls under the category of supplementary capital, in that it does not reflect ordinary business results. Because of this revaluation, reserves typically are not counted as capital that can be leveraged for financial institutions, such as a bank or contractual provisions.

The gain from a revaluation is called a surplus. It is **not** usually a profit because it is not taken through the profit and loss account and recognised as a profit. This is to prevent profits being distorted by one-off gains, obscuring trends in the business itself. A reduction in the value of an asset on revaluation (a deficit) is usually a loss.

A loss on a non-current asset reverses any previous surplus – reducing the revaluation reserve. The accounting treatment is the opposite of that for increments. The decrement is taken to the Statement of Changes in Equity if it can be offset against an existing revaluation reserve for that asset. Once the asset's revaluation reserve has been used, any further decrement is treated as an expense in the Income Statement ie a negative revaluation reserve is not permitted.

Special Reserves

At times, a company may create a reserve for a special purpose by transferring amounts from retained earnings to a special reserve account. For example an Asset Replacement Reserve – this reserve will accumulate funds, in addition to the amounts set aside as depreciation, to ensure there is enough funds available when the asset needs to be bought. These are really sub-divisions of the retained earnings account.

The paid up capital and reserves of a company make up the company's Shareholders' Funds.

Introduction to Statement in Changes in Equity

At the end of the financial year, between the amended Trial Balance and the Balance Sheet, there is a further financial statement that shows the detail of change in Owner's Equity between the previous financial year and the current financial year.

The Statement of Changes in Equity shows the changes that have taken place within the owner's claim on the business. The purpose of this statement is to show how the change in equity between the beginning of the accounting period and the end of the accounting period has occurred by:

Combining information about net surplus (deficit) with other aspects of an entity's financial performance [such as gains or losses from revaluing non-current assets] in order to give a measure of comprehensive income. In conjunction with the Statement of Financial Position, it also provides information that is useful for assessing the return on investment in the entity.

In the reconciliation of the equity at the beginning of the period with the equity at the end of the period, the following items must be disclosed separately in the Statement of Changes in Equity:

- original (opening) capital
- net profit (surplus) or net loss (deficit) from the Statement of Comprehensive Income
- any contributions made by the owner(s) –
  - additional capital invested into the business (for a sole trader or partnership)
  - subscribed for additional shares (in the case of companies)
- any distributions to the owners –
  - drawings (for a sole trader or partnership)
  - dividends (in the case of companies)
- increases/decreases in revaluation reserves – changes in the valuation of non-current assets or liabilities
- currency translation differences – changes in the value of investments in foreign operations caused by exchange rate fluctuations
- profit/loss on sale of book value of assets
- minority interests – if a company has a subsidiary that is not 100% owned, changes in the value of minority interests during the period must be disclosed
- adjustments for fundamental errors in opening equity – this should occur only infrequently if there has been an error in the calculation of equity in an earlier accounting period

Further information that will affect this financial statement will be adjustments that might include:

- stock taken by the owner
- borrowings to the owner (from the business)
- incorrect coding
- revaluation of non current assets

In summary – this statement shows the total owner's equity (stake in the business) at the beginning of the financial year and then details the changes that have taken place. This complies with and demonstrates the standard for Disclosure.

Why have a Statement of Changes in Equity?
- It shows the movement of activities as it relates to the Equity section of the Balance Sheet.
- It allows the Balance Sheet to be written up clearly and without unnecessary detail (which can still be accessed through the Statement of Changes in Equity and/or through Notes to the accounts.
- It gives a concise figure in the Equity section of the Balance Sheet.

The Link

The Statement of Changes in Equity is the link between the Income Statement and the Balance Sheet. The purpose is to show how the equity has changed from the start of the accounting period to the end of the accounting period.

It primarily tells us the changes taking place in the owner's equity and provides information that is useful for assessing the return on investment.

> My personal explanation of the need for a separate financial statement:
> - The Balance Sheet is a static document ie a snapshot of the business structure.
> - The Statement of Changes in Equity is showing the movements ie contributions, distributions, revaluations, foreign currency fluctuations etc and any like activities.
> - It also provides an easier statement face for the Balance Sheet by limiting the entries to: capital, retained earnings and asset revaluation reserves.

Under accounting standards, an entity should present a statement of changes in equity as a separate component of its financial statements or at least present it as a Note to the financial statements.

Sole Trader Examples

Task #1

Tim's Terrific Toys Limited
Statement of Changes in Equity
for the year ending 31 March 2018

	$	$	$
Opening equity	12,000		
add capital introduced	4,000		
add asset revaluation reserve	_____	16,000	
plus net profit	2,000		
less drawings	(500)	1,500	
Closing equity			17,500

Task #2

Lillian's Linen Store
Statement of Changes in Equity
for the year ending 31 March 2018

	$	$	$
Opening equity	25,000		
add capital introduced			
add asset revaluation reserve	_____	25,000	
plus net profit	17,000		
less drawings	(11,000)	6,000	
Closing equity			31,000

Task #3

Cathy's Catery
Statement of Changes in Equity
for the year ending 31 March 2018

	$	$	$
Opening equity	41,000		
add capital introduced	4,000		
add asset revaluation reserve	_____	45,000	
less net loss	(17,000)		
less drawings	(5,000)	(22,000)	
Closing equity			23,000

Task #4

Melody's Music
Statement of Changes in Equity
for the year ending 31 March 2018

	$	$	$
Opening equity	15,000		
add capital introduced			
add asset revaluation reserve	_____	15,000	
plus net profit	22,000		
less drawings	(2,000)	20,000	
Closing equity			35,000

Task #5

Pam's Pancakes
Statement of Changes in Equity
for the year ending 31 March 2018

	$	$	$
Opening equity	27,000		
add capital introduced	3,000		
add asset revaluation reserve	14,000	44,000	
plus net profit	10,000		
less drawings		10,000	
Closing equity			54,000

Task #6

Abby's Art Gallery
Statement of Changes in Equity
for the year ending 31 March 2018

	$	$	$
Opening equity	15,000		
add capital introduced	10,000		
add asset revaluation reserve		25,000	
less net loss	(14,000)		
less drawings	(2,000)	(16,000)	
Closing equity			9,000

Task #7

Alec's Aquarium
Statement of Changes in Equity
for the year ending 31 March 2018

	$	$	$
Opening equity			
add capital introduced	20,000		
add asset revaluation reserve		20,000	
plus net profit	12,000		
less drawings	(1,500)	10,500	
Closing equity			30,500

Task #8

Bert's Beehives
Statement of Changes in Equity
for the year ending 31 March 2018

	$	$	$
Opening equity	37,000		
add capital introduced	3,000		
add asset revaluation reserve	4,000	44,000	
plus net profit	16,000		
less drawings	(10,000)	6,000	
Closing equity			50,000

Introductory Tasks ~ Sole Trader

The following tasks are to demonstrate your understanding of the Proprietorship (Owner's Equity/Capital) layout of the Balance Sheet. For each task draw up the appropriate layout.

Task #1

Helen Clark has run a part-time dress shop called Costume Garments for a couple of years now. At 31 March 2018 she had made a net profit of $41,000 which she is very pleased about. At the start of the financial year (1 April 2017) she had capital of $58,000. During the financial year, her shop was by QV and assessed to be worth another $25,000. There have been a few times during the year that she has had to "draw" on her funds when her pay from her full-time job was not sufficient. These drawings amount to $17,000.

Task #2

Cy Rill started up a corner dairy on 1 April 2017 with an investment of $25,000. During the year he drew, from the business, $1,000 a month for his own use. As the business was slow to get up and running he had to put another $4,000 worth of capital into the dairy. Business has slowly improved but the profit was only $14,000. Hopefully at 31 March 2018, he is still in a better situation than at the start of the year!

Task #3

Flora runs a flower shop called Flowermaids. Apart from flowers she also runs a side business selling 'fancifuls' – flower related items. Business has been gradually getting better each year as her customers recommend her shop to others. The 2018 financial year was exceptionally busy and she earned after taxes $45,000. At 1 April 2017, her capital in the business was $50,000. During the year she inherited some money and decided to invest $12,000 of it in the business. She also put her car into the business name (it had a valuation of $7,000). This will allow her to claim more easily when she makes deliveries. Flora gave herself a salary (shown as drawings) of $2,100 per month.

Solutions ~ Sole Trader Tasks

Solution ~ Task #1

Costume Garments
Statement of Changes in Equity
for the year ending 31 March 2018

	$	$	$
Opening equity	58,000		
add capital introduced	0		
add asset revaluation reserve	25,000	83,000	
plus net profit	41,000		
less drawings	(17,000)	24,000	
Closing equity			**107,000**

Solution ~ Task #2

Cy Rill
Statement of Changes in Equity
for the year ending 31 March 2018

	$	$	$
Opening equity	25,000		
add capital introduced	4,000		
add asset revaluation reserve		29,000	
plus net profit	14,000		
less drawings	(12,000)	2,000	
Closing equity			**31,000**

Solution ~ Task #3

Flowermaids
Statement of Changes in Equity
for the year ending 31 March 2018

	$	$	$
Opening equity	50,000		
add capital introduced	19,000	69,000	
add asset revaluation reserve			
plus net profit	45,000		
less drawings	25,200	19,800	
Closing Equity			**88,800**

Partnerships Examples

There are a number of ways of showing the changes from one financial year to another for partnerships:
- Sometimes capital is shown with all the changes that have occurred throughout the year.
- Sometimes capital is kept separate – that is, it remains 'fixed' and a **current account** is where the year's changes appear. In this case, the capital does not change from one year to the next – unless a partner adds to that capital.

The current account shows:
- The transactions such as drawings, salaries, profit and interest received on both the capital and current accounts.
- The balance of the current account will fluctuate each year.
- The balance can be either credit or debit.

Either option is acceptable – it has to work for the partnership itself.

Here are two examples just using the capital account:

Example #1:

Khloe and Kendal Klothing
Statement of Changes in Equity
for year ended 30 June 2018

	Khloe	Kendal	Total
Capital, 1 July 2017	50,000	35,000	85,000
Additional Investment	4,000	0	4,000
Net Profit	44,660	32,340	77,000
Subtotal:	98,660	67,340	166,000
less Withdrawals	28,000	35,000	63,000
Capital, 30 June 2018	**70,660**	**32,340**	**103,000**

Profit Distribution based on capital investment:		
Khloe	51,000	58%
Kendal	37,000	42%
	88,000	

Profit for financial year:	77,000	77,000*.58
Khloe	44,660	77,000*.42
Kendal	32,340	

This is just how I dealt with the background detail to let you see how I arrived at the figures. Do not include in the Statement of Changes in Equity.

Khloe and Kendal Klothing
Statement of Changes in Equity
for year ended 30 June 2018
(extract)

Capital		
Khloe	70,660	
Kendal	32,340	103,000

Example #2:

Bill and Ben Florists
Statement of Changes in Equity
for year ended 31 March 2018

	Bill	Ben	Total
Capital, 1 April 2017	27,000	40,000	67,000
Additional Investment	5,000	5,000	10,000
Net Profit	22,000	33,000	55,000
Subtotal:	54,000	78,000	132,000
less Withdrawals	17,000	12,000	29,000
Capital, 31 March 2018	**37,000**	**66,000**	**103,000**

Profit Distribution based on capital investment:

Bill	27,000	40%
Ben	40,000	60%
	67,000	

Profit for financial year:	55,000	
Bill	22,000	55,000*.40
Ben	33,000	55,000*.60

This is just how I dealt with the background detail to let you see how I arrived at the figures. Do not include in the Statement of Changes in Equity.

Bill and Ben Florists
Statement of Changes in Equity
for year ended 31 March 2018
(extract)

Capital		
Bill	37,000	
Ben	66,000	103,000

Notes:

- In order for me to work out the percentage amount that each partner should receive from the profits, I total the opening capital and then put each partner's capital contribution over that figure. I have shown this below:

	Partner 1	Partner 2	Total Capital
Capital	25,000	40,000	65,000
	25,000/65,000 = 38%	40,000/65,000 = 62%	

- Sometimes though the percentage return from profits is not decided on contributed capital but rather decided by the partners when they put their partnership agreement together. Examples:
  - One partner may have contributed no capital but is a 'working' partner while the other partner(s) may be 'silent' – invested capital but do not actually work in the partnership.
  - Both partners have invested the same amount of capital but one of the partners may have had more experience of the business, or has brought in clients from a previous partnership.

Partnership Tasks ~ Capital Account only

The following tasks are to demonstrate the layouts for a partnership where the capital account is the only account used to record the changes in equity from year to year.

Task #1

Ally McBeal and Kylie Minnogue decide to go into partnership, as equal partners, to run a pet shop. They both contribute $21,000 on 1 April 2017. During the year, Kylie withdrew $5,000. The profit for the year was $8,000. Calculate the capital for each as at 31 March 2018.

Task #2

In April 2017 Sally and Adam invest in a surf shop. Sally contributes $20,000 and Adam contributes $34,000. Profits are paid into each partner's Current Account based on their capital contribution. Profits were good during the year: $40,000. How much did each receive in profit and what is each partner's equity as at 31 March 2018?

Task #3

Gerald Khan and Jeremy Kannnot are partners in a nightclub. When the partnership was established it was decided that Gerald should receive 65% of the profits and Jeremy 35%. This was based on the fact that Gerald had been in the nightclub business for many years and had the experience whilst Jeremy's background was more as a customer. At 1 April 2017 the capital for both was $50,000. There were no drawings taken during the year by Gerald, but Jeremy withdrew $2,000. Profit was $82,000. Itemise the individual partner's details as at 31 March 2018.

Solutions ~ Partnership Tasks (Capital Account only)

Solution ~ Task #1

Ally and Kylie
Pet Shop
Statement in Changes in Equity for year ended 31 March 2018

	$	$	$
Equity			
Ally			
Capital 1 April 2017	21,000		
plus profit	4,000		
less drawings			
Capital 31 March 2018		25,000	
Kylie			
Capital 1 April 2017	21,000		
plus profit	4,000		
less drawings	5,000		
Capital 31 March 2018		20,000	$45,000

Solution ~ Task #2

Surf Shop

	$	$	$
Proprietorship			
Capital 31 March 2018			
Sally	20,000		
Adam	34,000	54,000	
Current Account 31 March 2018			
Sally	14,815		
Adam	25,185	40,000	
			94,000

Calculation for percentage each has contributed in capital to the business:

Total Contribution at 1 April 2017		54,000	
Sally	20,000/54,000	0.37037	37%
Adam	34,000/54,000	0.62963	63%

Profit: 40,000

Solution ~ Task #3

Night Club

	$	$	$
Equity			
Capital 1 April 2017 - Gerard Khan	50,000		
plus profit	53,300		
	103,300		
less drawings	_____		
Capital 31 March 2018		103,300	
Capital 1 April 2017 - Jeremy Kannot	50,000		
plus profit	28,700		
	78,700		
less drawings	2,000		
Capital 31 March 2018		76,700	
			180,000

Profit Calculation:
Profit   82,000
           Gerard   65%
           Jeremy   35%

Partnership ~ Capital and Current Accounts

Dealing with the partnership changes in equity is a little more involved, because there is usually a partnership agreement that details how much interest etc each partner receives and how much of the year's profit they will be allocated. With a partnership, profit is usually called surplus. If there is no partnership agreement, the law dictates equal proportion allocations. I have provided you with a detailed step by step method of dealing with this format.

Notes:
- Profit is usually referred to as surplus in a partnership.
- Capital contributions do not change from year to year, unless the partner adds or withdraws from their capital.
- All the working out occurs in the Current Account – think of this as the 'movement' that equates to the Statement of Changes in Equity (for a company).

Worked Task

C & D Partners

C & D Partners are involved in education resources.

For the year ended 31 March 2018 the profit before allocation was $69,800.

The partnership deed specifies:
- interest of 10% on Capital account
- interest of 5% on Current account
- no salary to be received by either partner
- balance of surplus to be allocated 50/50

Balances as at 1 April 2017:
- Capital Accounts –

    Colin $20,000
    Daisy $90,000

- Current Accounts –

    Colin $7,600
    Daisy $5,800

- Drawings for year –

    Colin $80 per week
    Daisy $90 per week

> This is where the interest received on the capital and current accounts is entered into the books, what salaries have been paid, as well as allocating to each of the partners, the residue of the surplus.

> This is the Statement of Changes in Equity for a partnership. It is only the Current account that is affected, but shows what has been added (interest and surplus) and what has been withdrawn (drawings).

Required to:
- Prepare the Appropriation Statement for the year ended 31 March 2018.
- Prepare a Schedule of Current Accounts for the year ended 31 March 2018.
- Prepare the Equity section of the Balance Sheet as at 31 March 2018.

C & D Partners

	Partners	
	Colin	Daisy
Capital at 1 April 2017	20,000	90,000
Current Accounts at 1 April 2017	7,600	5,800
Drawings for the year	4,160	4,680
Surplus for the year		**69,800**

The partnership deed provides the following details:

	Colin	Daisy
Salaries	0	0
Interest on:		
Capital Account	10%	10%
Current Account	5%	5%
Residue of Surplus	50%	50%

Profit Allocation between the partners of Colin and Daisy for year ended 31 March 2018

	$	$	$
Surplus			69,800
Interest			
Contributed Capital			
Colin	2,000		
Daisy	9,000	11,000	
Current Account			
Colin	380		
Daisy	290	670	
Salaries			
Colin	0		
Daisy	0	0	11,670
			58,130
Share of Surplus			
Colin	29,065		
Daisy	29,065	58,130	**69,800**

Statement of Changes in Equity in Current Accounts for the year ended 31 March 2018

Current Accounts	Colin	Daisy	Total
Opening Balance	7,600	5,800	13,400
			0
Interest:			0
Contributed Capital	2,000	9,000	11,000
Current Accounts	380	290	670
			0
Salaries	0	0	0
			0
Residue of Surplus	29,065	29,065	58,130
	39,045	44,155	83,200
less Drawings	4,160	4,680	8,840
Closing Balance	**$34,885**	**$39,475**	**$74,360**

C & D Partners
Balance Sheet as at 31 March 2018

Extract Only

	$	$	$
Equity			
Colin			
Contributed Capital	20,000		
Current Account	34,885	54,885	
Daisy			
Contributed Capital	90,000		
Current Account	39,475	129,475	**$184,360**

Statement in Changes in Equity

Partnership Tasks ~ Capital and Current Accounts

The following tasks are to demonstrate the layouts for a partnership where the capital account is kept separate from the current (ongoing from year to year) account.

Task #1

Luke and Larry are lawyers who set up in their own practice a few years' ago. They each contributed $15,000 of capital into the practice. They drew up a partnership agreement (as you would expect being lawyers). In this partnership deed:

- Each would receive $40,000 a year in salary.
- Interest on the capital account would be 7%.
- Interest on the current account would be 5%.
- Residue of surplus would be 65% for Luke and 35% for Larry. The rationale for this, was that Luke had been practising law for many years and had brought in the majority of clients to the practice while Larry was still learning (although qualified of course). This allocation would be changed within the near future.

During the year, Luke withdrew $4,000 as drawings. The surplus for the year was $117,850.

Prepare for 31 March 2018:
- Profit allocation worksheet.
- Statement of Changes in Equity in the Current account.
- Balance Sheet extract for the equity section.

Task #2

In April 2016, Simon, Callum and Freddy went into a partnership to run a gardening service. They called it Gardeners 3. They had allocated a role for each of them in the business. Each contributed $10,000 of capital. The balance of their current accounts as at 1 April 2017 is:
Simon - $22,000
Callum - $17,000
Freddy - $19,000

Their partnership agreement is shown below:
- Interest on capital – 4%
- Interest on current account – 5%
- Profits to be divided equally
- Salary for each of $27,000 per annum.

During the year, Simon had drawings of $8,400 and Freddy had drawings of $11,000. The business had a net surplus of $100,000 for the end of the 2018 financial year.

Prepare for 31 March 2018:
- Profit allocation worksheet.
- Statement of Changes in Equity in the Current account.
- Balance Sheet extract for the equity section.

Solutions ~ Partnership Tasks (Capital and Current)

Solution ~ Task #1

Luke and Larry Lawyers

	Partners		
	Luke	Larry	
	$	$	$
Capital at 1 April 2017	15,000	15,000	
Current Accounts at 1 April 2017	52,000	24,500	106,500
Drawings for the year	4,000	0	
Surplus for the year	117,850		

Profit Allocation between the partners of Luke and Larry for year ended 31 March 2018

	$	$	$
Surplus			117,850
Interest			
Contributed Capital			
Luke	1,050		
Larry	1,050	2,100	
Current Account			
Luke	2,600		
Larry	1,225	3,825	
Salaries			
Luke	40,000		
Larry	40,000	80,000	85,925
			31,925
Share of Surplus			
Luke	20,751		
Larry	11,174	31,925	117,850

Statement of Changes in Equity in Current Accounts
for the year ended 31 March 2018

Current Accounts	Luke	Larry	Total
Opening Balance	52,000	24,500	76,500
Interest:			
Contributed Capital	1,050	1,050	2,100
Current Accounts	2,600	1,225	3,825
Salaries	40,000	40,000	80,000
Residue of Surplus	20,751	11,174	31,925
	116,401	77,949	194,350
less Drawings	4,000	0	4,000
Closing Balance	**$112,401**	**$77,949**	**$190,350**

Luke and Larry Lawyers
Balance Sheet as at 31 March 2018

Extract Only

	$	$	$
Equity			
Luke			
Contributed Capital	15,000		
Current Account	112,401	127,401	
Larry			
Contributed Capital	15,000		
Current Account	77,949	92,949	**$220,350**

Solution ~ Task #2

Gardeners 3

	Simon $	Partners Callum $	Freddy $
Capital at 1 April 2017	10,000	10,000	10,000
Current Accounts at 1 April 2017	22,000	17,000	19,000
Drawings for the year	8,400	0	11,000

Profit Allocation between the partners of Simon, Callum and Freddy for year ended 31 March 2018

	$	$	$
Surplus			100,000
Interest			
Contributed Capital			
Simon	400		
Callum	400		
Freddy	400	1,200	
Current Account			
Simon	1,100		
Callum	850		
Freddy	950	2,900	
Salaries			
Simon	27,000		
Callum	27,000		
Freddy	27,000	81,000	85,100
			14,900
Share of Surplus			
Simon	4,967		
Callum	4,967		
Freddy	4,967	14,900	100,000

Statement of Changes in Equity in Current Accounts for the year ended 31 March 2018

Current Accounts	Simon	Callum	Freddy	Total
Opening Balance	22,000	17,000	19,000	58,000
Interest:				
Contributed Capital	400	400	400	1,200
Current Accounts	1,100	850	950	2,900
Salaries	27,000	27,000	27,000	81,000
Residue of Surplus	4,967	4,967	4,967	14,900
	55,467	50,217	52,317	158,000
less Drawings	8,400	0	11,000	19,400
Closing Balance	**$47,067**	**$50,217**	**$41,317**	**$138,600**

Gardeners 3
Balance Sheet as at 31 March 2018
Extract Only

	$	$	$
Equity			
Simon			
Contributed Capital	10,000		
Current Account	47,067	57,067	
Callum			
Contributed Capital	10,000		
Current Account	50,217	60,217	
Freddy			
Contributed Capital	10,000		
Current Account	41,317	51,317	**$168,600**

Company Examples

Wellie Limited

Example Extract

Wellie Limited
Balance Sheet
as at 30 June 2013

Equity	
Contributed Capital	
Issued and paid up Capital	
50,000 10% preference shares of $1 fully paid	50,000
80,000 ordinary shares of $1 paid to 80 cents	64,000
	114,000
Other Equity	
Retained Earnings	80,000
Asset Revaluation Reserve	15,000
	209,000
Less dividends of 10 % payable in cash – ordinary shares	6,400
Total Equity	**$202,600**

> **Retained Earnings** – represent surpluses arising from trading activities that have not been distributed to the owners. Instead, these surpluses are retained in the business and may be used to increase working capital, reduce debt or to finance capital expenditure.

Recognising Dividends

Dividends are the equivalent of sole trader drawings. They are based on so many cents per share held. Include interim and final dividends.

Interim dividends are paid during the year.

Final dividends are usually declared at the end of the year but paid after the end of the year.

Dividends are recognised when the solvency test is met and the solvency certificate has been signed.

Final Dividends

- Dividends proposed or declared before balance date but not authorised for payment until after balance date are not recognised in the financial statements.
- These are disclosed in the Notes to the financial statements.
- They are considered to be an event after the reporting period.
- Will be recognised in the financial statements in the year that they are paid.

> **Distributions** – usually occurs in one of two ways:
> - An interim dividend is usually declared and paid before the end of the accounting period (regarded as a distribution in anticipation of surpluses). The final dividend is normally recommended by the directors and approved by the shareholders at the AGM and takes into account any interim dividends which may have been distributed.
> - In the form of a bonus issue of shares, that results in the conversion of reserves into contributed capital which is usually allocated to existing shareholders on the basis of existing shares held.

Layouts

Business Name
Statement of Changes in Equity
for the year ended ...

Total shareholders equity at the start of year (total from Balance Sheet)	x
Add	
NPAT	x
Further shares issued	x
Increases in revaluation of assets	x
Less	
Dividends paid to shareholders	(x)
Net losses	(x)
Decreases in revaluation reserves	(x)
Shareholders' equity at end of financial period	x

Updating the equity section of the Balance Sheet

Business Name
Balance Sheet
as at ...

Equity

Issued capital (opening balance + further shares issued)	x
Retained earnings (opening balance + NPAT less dividends paid out)	x
Asset revaluation reserves (opening balance + increases – decreases)	x
Equity at the end of the year	x

Note:
The equity at the end must balance to the equity at the end in the Statement of Changes in Equity.

Statement in Changes in Equity

Company Worked Task

Marchionette Limited has provided you with the following figures for the year ended 31 March 2018. Prepare the Statement of Changes in Equity.

Depreciation not applicable to this statement; and 'proposed' dividend is not 'actual' dividend.

Increase in asset revaluation reserve	80,000	Depreciation	43,000
Net surplus before tax	213,000	Opening equity	2,873,600
Final dividend proposed	50,000	Interim dividend paid	25,000
Income tax payable	70,290	Paid up capital	2,000,000
Asset revaluation reserve	168,000	Share issue during year	500,000

Marchionette Limited
Statement of Changes in Equity
for year ended 31 March 2018

Net surplus after tax	142,710
Increase in asset revaluation reserve	80,000
Total recognised revenue and expenses	222,710
Contributions from owners:	
Paid up capital	500,000
Distributions to owners:	
Dividend paid	25,000
Change in equity for the year	697,710
Equity at start of year	2,873,600
Equity at end of year	3,571,310
Final dividend proposed for year	50,000

Further Worked Example

Ken's Furniture Limited
Statement of Changes in Equity
for the year ended 31 March 2018

Shareholders funds at the start of the year		7,900,000
Add		
NPAT		441,000
Increase in ARR		200,000
Increase in share capital		1,000,000
		9,541,000
Deduct		
Dividends		125,000
Decrease in ARR		
Shareholders funds at the end of the year		9,416,000

Ken's Furniture Limited **Balance Sheet as at 31 March 2018**

Shareholders Funds		
Issued capital	6,000,000	
Retained earnings	3,066,000	
ARR	350,000	9,416,000

Further Examples

Beeswax Limited

Beeswax Limited had the following equity at 1 April 2017:
retained earnings 352,800
100,000 ordinary shares 2,800,000
asset revaluation reserves 10,500

Equity	1 April 2017			
		shares	2,800,000	
		retained earnings	352,800	
		asset revaluation reserves	10,000	3,162,800
During the year:				
opening equity				3,162,800
net surplus after tax was recorded			141,500	
final dividend paid			(25,200)	116,300
				3,279,100
Equity	31 March 2018			
		shares	2,800,000	
		retained earnings	469,100	
		asset revaluation reserve	10,000	
				3,279,100

Albatross Limited

Albatross Limited had the following equity at 1 April 2017:
retained earnings 72,000
100,000 ordinary shares @ $4.50
asset revaluation reserves 110,500

Equity	1 April 2017			
		shares	450,000	
		retained earnings	72,000	
		asset revaluation reserves	110,500	632,500
During the year:				
opening equity				632,500
net surplus after tax was recorded			152,000	
final dividend			(15,000)	
interim dividend			(8,700)	128,300
GV revalued land from 800,000 to 970,000				170,000
				930,800
Equity	31 March 2018			
		shares	450,000	
		retained earnings	200,300	
		asset revaluation reserve	280,500	930,800

Company Tasks # 1 – 6

Task #1 ~ Eastern Traders Ltd

At balance date of 30 June 2018, the following balances were included in the Trial Balance of Eastern Traders Ltd:

issued capital 300,000 ordinary shares (1/7/17)	$300,000
retained earnings	$69,500
asset revaluation reserve (1/7/17)	$25,000

Other information relating to the year ending 30 June 2018:
- taxation to be calculated at 30%
- final dividend for previous year paid at 8 cents per share
- interim dividend for current year paid out in total — $10,000
- goodwill — $40,000
- net profit before taxation (for year ending 30/6/18) — $78,400

Required
- Prepare the Statement of Changes in Equity for the year ending 30 June 2018.
- Update and prepare the Shareholders funds section of the Balance Sheet as at 30 June 2018.

Task #2 ~ Sunfield Industries Ltd

The equity section of Sunfield Industries Ltd as at 1 April 2017 is shown below:

share capital 1 million shares @ $2	$2,000,000
retained earnings	$500,000
asset revaluation reserve - land	$150,000
asset revaluation reserve – buildings	$20,000

Other information relating to the year ending 31 March 2018:
- profit for the year was $400,000
- company income tax – 28 cents in the dollar
- final dividend paid out in June 2017 for the 2016 year @ 8 cents per share
- interim dividend paid in October 2017 @ 10 cents per share
- land revalued from $500,000 to $630,000
- 50,000 fully paid shares issued at a share price of $1.00 on 1 January 2012

Required
- Prepare the Statement of Changes in Equity for the year ending 31 March 2018.
- Prepare the Shareholders funds section of the Balance Sheet as at 31 March 2018.

Task #3 ~ Mac Merrin Ltd

The Shareholders' Funds section of the Balance Sheet for Mac Merrin Ltd as at 1 April 2017 is as follows:

share capital 100,000 ordinary shares @ $2.50	
retained earnings	$123,000
asset revaluation reserve – four buildings	$50,000

During the financial year ending 31 March 2018, the company:

- made a profit before tax of $420,000
- tax rate at 28%
- paid in August 2017, previous year's final dividend of 11 cents per share
- paid in January 2018, an interim dividend for this year of 9 cents per share
- during the year received a revaluation of the land up by $25,000
- issued in February 2018, a further 90,000 shares for $3.50 cash
- sold one of the buildings (which had been previously revalued upward by $20,000) for $25,000 at a loss on its book value of $38,000.

Required

- Prepare the Statement of Changes in Equity for the year ending 31 March 2018.
- Prepare the Shareholders funds section of the Balance Sheet as at 31 March 2018.

Task #4 ~ Ratu Limited

The equity section of Ratu Limited as at 1 April 2017 is shown below:

share capital 100,000 shares	$150,000
retained earnings	$30,000
asset revaluation reserve - building	$20,000

Other information relating to the year ending 31 March 2018:

- profit for the year before tax was $100,000
- calculate tax at 30%
- dividends paid during the year - $10,000:
- sold building for $140,000 (book value of $170,000) – building had previously been revalued upward
- purchase of fixed assets - $200,000
- land revalued from $50,000 to $90,000

Required

- Prepare the Statement of Changes in Equity for the year ending 31 March 2018.
- Update and prepare the Shareholders funds section of the Balance Sheet as at 31 March 2018.

Task #5 ~ Harlequin Products Ltd

The Shareholders' Funds section of the Balance Sheet for Harlequin Products Ltd as at 1 April 2017 is as follows:

share capital 400,000 ordinary shares	$1,020,000
retained earnings	$410,000
asset revaluation reserve	$370,000
Total Shareholders' Funds	$1,800,000

During the financial year ending 31 March 2018, the company:
- made a profit before tax of $590,000 – tax rate of 30%
- paid in July 2017 the previous year's final dividend of 7 cents per share
- paid in December 2017, an interim dividend for this year of 5 cents per share
- land was revalued from $290,000 to $440,000
- a building purchased in 2012 for $55,000 and with accumulated depreciation of $30,000 was sold for $40,000 during the financial year
- in February 2018, the company issued a further 100,000 shares for $3.40 cash (fully paid on allotment)

Required
- Prepare the Statement of Changes in Equity for the year ending 31 March 2018.
- Update and prepare the Shareholders Funds section of the Balance Sheet as at 31 March 2018.

Task 6 ~ Palladian Pottery Limited

This is a closely held company with five family members as shareholders. The company has been in existence for 12 years and has slowly increased its equity.

At the end of the 2017 financial year, the Balance Sheet showed the following breakdown of the family's investment in the business:

issued capital – 150,000 $1.50 ordinary shares	$225,000
retained earnings	$118,110
asset revaluation reserve (land $217,000, buildings $75,000)	$292,000

Financial information relating to the financial year ending 31 March 2018:

profit	$300,500
tax rate @ 28%)	
shares purchased in a local utility company (purchased April 2017)	$140,000
final dividend (for 2016) paid out in June 2017	7 cents per share
interim dividend paid out in December 2017	2 cents per share
land revalued in August 2017 by	$120,000
equipment purchased in September 2017	$300,000
further shares issued for cash in October 2017	100,000 shares @ $2.00 each
buildings devalued during the financial year	$37,000

Required:
- Prepare the Statement of Changes in Equity for the year ended 31 March 2018.
- Prepare the Shareholders' Funds section of the Balance Sheet as at 31 March 2018.

Solutions ~ Company Tasks #1 – 5

Solution ~ Eastern Traders

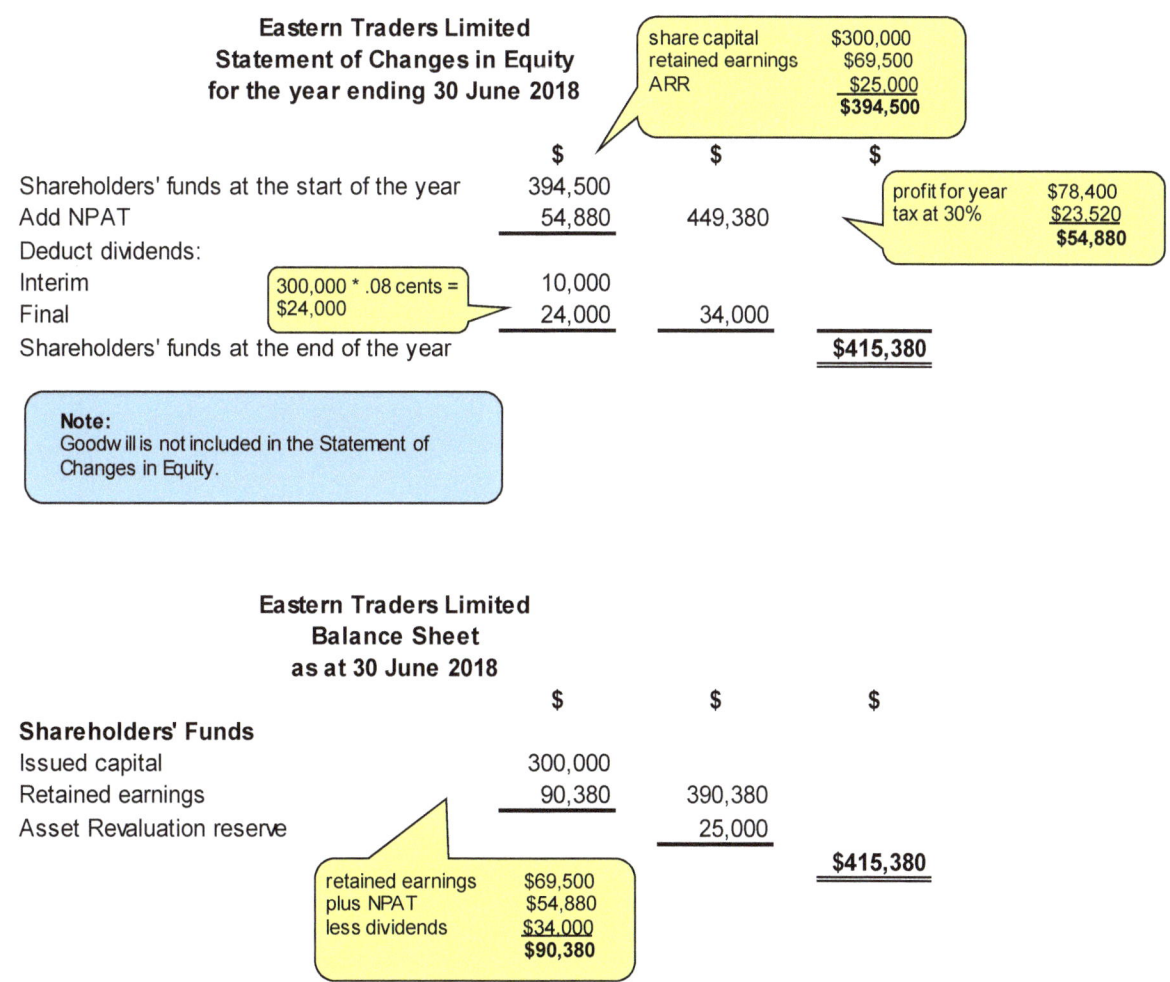

Eastern Traders Limited
Statement of Changes in Equity
for the year ending 30 June 2018

share capital $300,000
retained earnings $69,500
ARR $25,000
$394,500

	$	$	$
Shareholders' funds at the start of the year	394,500		
Add NPAT	54,880	449,380	
Deduct dividends:			
Interim	10,000		
Final	24,000	34,000	
Shareholders' funds at the end of the year			$415,380

300,000 * .08 cents = $24,000

profit for year $78,400
tax at 30% $23,520
$54,880

Note:
Goodwill is not included in the Statement of Changes in Equity.

Eastern Traders Limited
Balance Sheet
as at 30 June 2018

	$	$	$
Shareholders' Funds			
Issued capital		300,000	
Retained earnings		90,380	390,380
Asset Revaluation reserve			25,000
			$415,380

retained earnings $69,500
plus NPAT $54,880
less dividends $34,000
$90,380

Solution ~ Sunfield Industries Ltd

Equity 1 April 2017

share capital (1,000,000 shares @ $2)		2,000,000	
retained earnings		500,000	
asset revaluation reserve - land	150,000		
asset revaluation reserve - building	20,000	170,000	**$2,670,000**

Sunfield Industries Limited
Statement of Changes in Equity
for year ended 31 March 2018

Equity			2,670,000
Profit	400,000		
tax @28%	112,000	288,000	
Final dividend paid out (June 2017) for 2016 year @ 8 cents per share	80,000		
Interim dividend paid out (October 2017) @ 10 cents per share	100,000	108,000	
Revaluation - land (revalued from 500,000 to 630,000)		130,000	
Shares issued - 50,000 @ $1.00 on 1 January 2018		50,000	
			$2,958,000
Equity 31 March 2018			
share capital (1,050,000 shares)		2,050,000	
retained earnings		608,000	
asset revaluation reserve		300,000	**$2,958,000**

Note (callout):
retained earnings 2017 $500,000
profit (after tax) $288,000
   $788,000
less dividends $80,000
   $100,000 $180,000
   $608,000

Solution ~ Mac Merrin Limited

		$	$
Equity 1 April 2017			
share capital (1,000,000 shares @ $2.50)		2,500,000	
retained earnings		123,000	
asset revaluation reserve - buildings		50,000	$2,673,000

Mac Merrin Limited
Statement of Changes in Equity
for year ended 31 March 2018

	$	$	$
Equity 1 April 2017			2,673,000
Equity			
Profit	420,000		
tax @28%	117,600	302,400	
Final dividend paid out (August 2017) for 2016 year @ 11 cents per share		110,000	
Interim dividend paid out - January 2018 @ 9 cents per share		90,000	102,400
Revaluation - land	25,000		
Shares issued - 90,000 @ 3.50 each	315,000	340,000	
Loss on book value of previously revalued building		20,000	320,000
			$3,095,400

> **Note:**
> Cannot claim the loss on the sale of the fixed asset (one of the buildings) - that will be shown in the Income Statement. However, you need to remove the asset revaluation amount for that asset out of the ARR account. In this case - the $20,000 that it had previously been revalued at.

Equity 31 March 2018		
share capital (1,090,000 shares)	2,815,000	
retained earnings	225,400	
asset revaluation reserve	55,000	$3,095,400

Original $50,000, less $20,000 for building removed

Solution ~ Ratu Limited

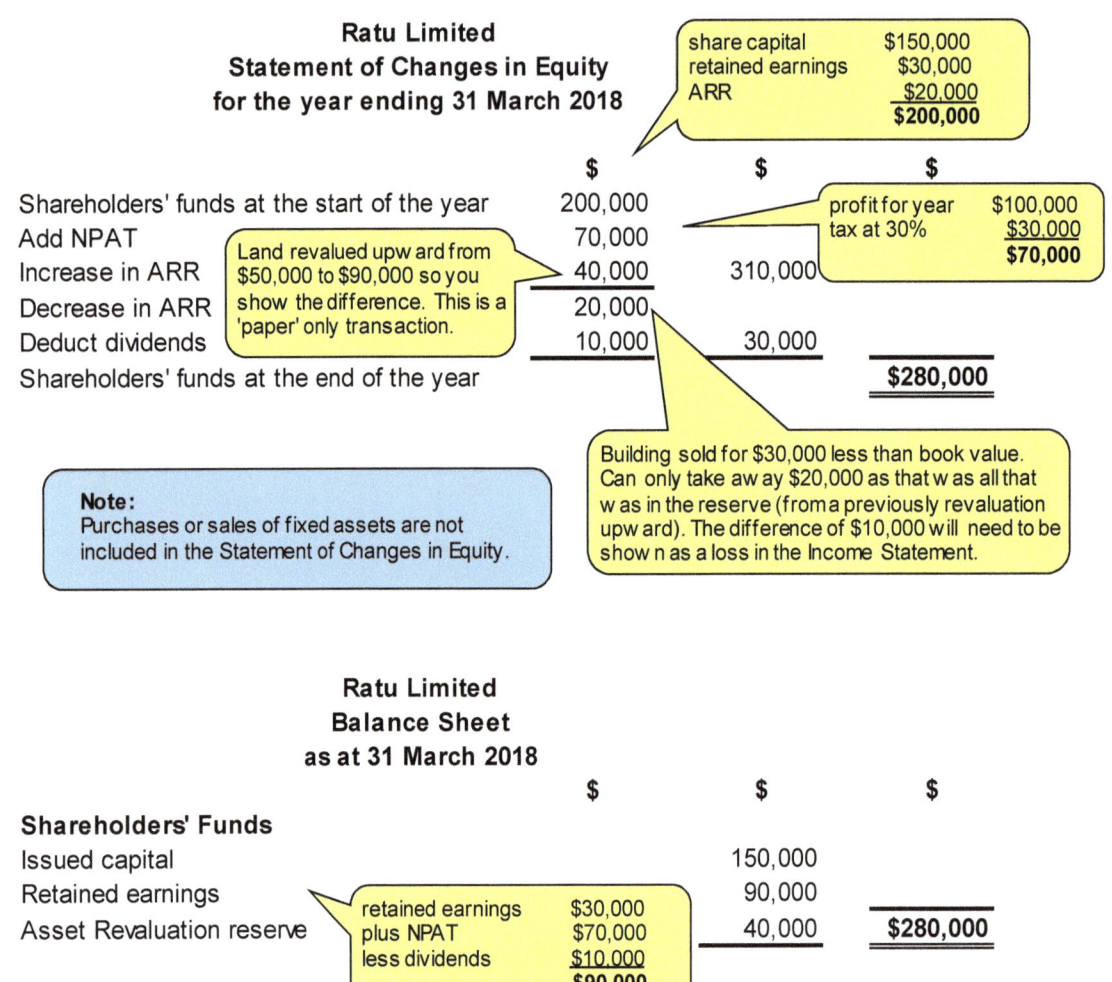

Solution ~ Harlequin Products Ltd

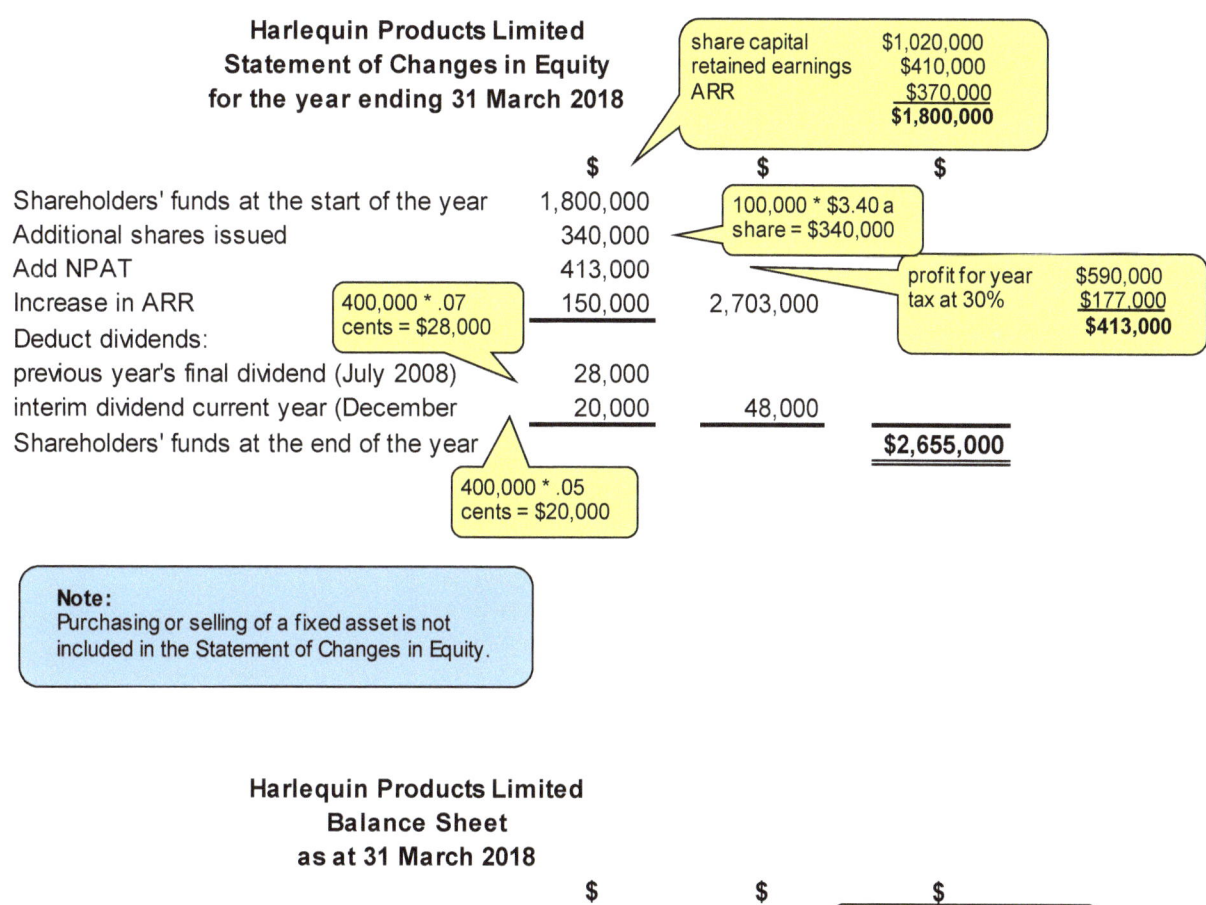

Harlequin Products Limited
Statement of Changes in Equity
for the year ending 31 March 2018

	$	$	$
Shareholders' funds at the start of the year	1,800,000		
Additional shares issued	340,000		
Add NPAT	413,000		
Increase in ARR	150,000	2,703,000	
Deduct dividends:			
previous year's final dividend (July 2008)	28,000		
interim dividend current year (December	20,000	48,000	
Shareholders' funds at the end of the year			$2,655,000

Callouts:
- share capital $1,020,000; retained earnings $410,000; ARR $370,000; $1,800,000
- 100,000 * $3.40 a share = $340,000
- profit for year $590,000; tax at 30% $177,000; $413,000
- 400,000 * .07 cents = $28,000
- 400,000 * .05 cents = $20,000

Note: Purchasing or selling of a fixed asset is not included in the Statement of Changes in Equity.

Harlequin Products Limited
Balance Sheet
as at 31 March 2018

	$	$	$
Shareholders' Funds			
Issued capital	1,360,000		
Retained earnings	775,000	2,135,000	
Asset Revaluation reserve		520,000	
			$2,655,000

Callouts:
- $1,020,000 plus $340,000 = $1,360,000
- retained earnings $410,000; plus NPAT $413,000; less dividends $48,000; $775,000

Solution ~ Palladian Pottery

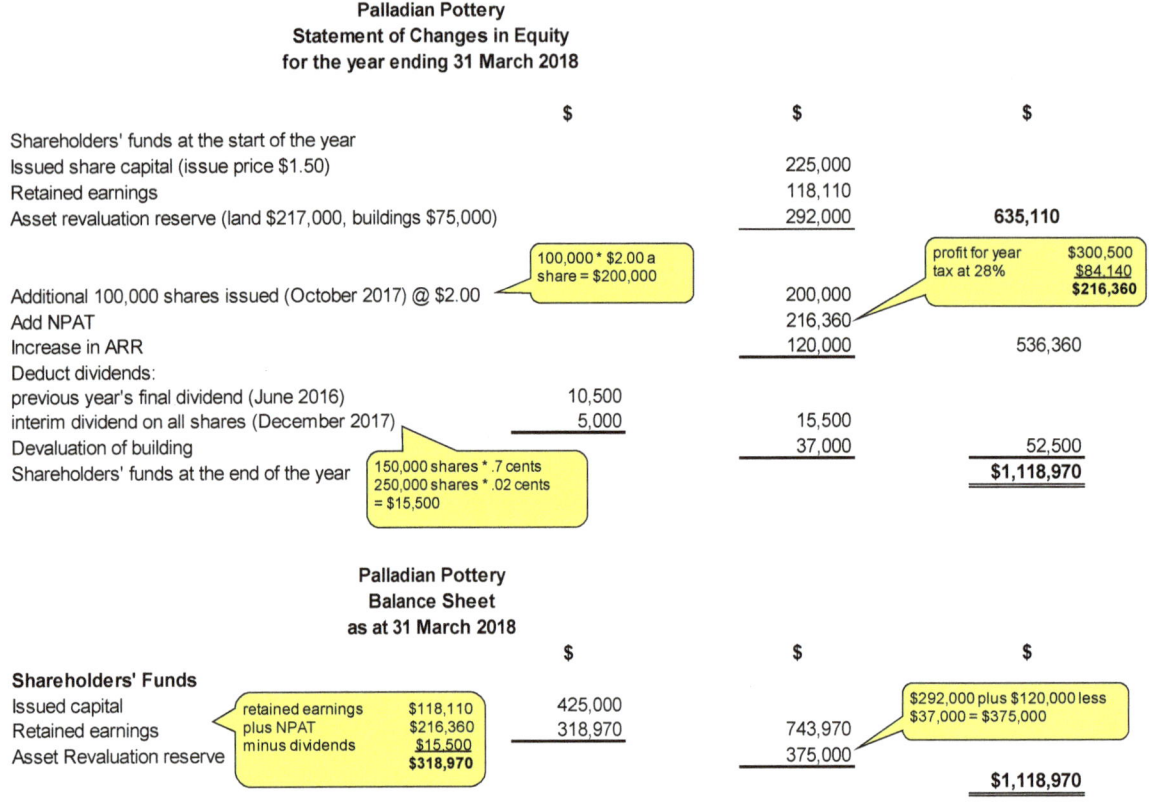

Notes:
- Purchasing shares in another business does not affect changes in equity.
- Purchasing of assets does not affect changes in equity.
- However, if an asset is sold and it had been revalued in some previous financial period, then that amount would need to be taken out of the asset revaluation reserve.
- Always keep in mind the following:
  - Declared dividends are not actually paid out dividends so should be ignored for the purposes of the Statement of Changes in Equity. They may (and usually are) declared in their current financial year, but can only be approved by the directors after the end of the financial year when the 'books' are analysed and the proof that the company can actually afford to pay out the dividend. This also links to the accounting rules of asset testing for company viability.
- That final dividends belong to the previous year and are included first.
- Interim dividends are the 'ongoing' dividends of the current financial year.

Worksheet Method for a Company

An alternative approach to the calculating the changes in equity especially for a company is the 'worksheet' method. I find this useful:
- to check the balances
- use this and then transfer the figures into the formal layout of the Statement of Changes in Equity
- sometimes I use it as just as a cross check when my figures do not balance!!

Will use the following task to demonstrate this method.

Then you might like to try it out on some of the tasks you have already completed.

If you were to use the worksheet for a sole trader business, you would replace dividends with drawings and instead of additional shares, it would probably show contributed capital.

Rum and Raisin
Statement of Changes in Equity
for the year ended 31 March 2014

	Capital	R/E	ARR	Total
Opening balances	77,000			77,000
Introduced capital	20,000			20,000
profit after tax		88,502		88,502
drawings		-28,270		-28,270
asset revalued			42,590	42,590
	97,000	**60,232**	**42,590**	**199,822**

Washdyke Tilers Limited

The Shareholders funds of the Balance Sheet of Washdyke Tilers Limited shows the following balances as at 1 April 2017:

Issued Capital	1,000,000
(500,000 ordinary shares)	
Retained Earnings	1,035,132
Asset Revaluation Reserve	150,000
Total Shareholders' Funds	2,185,132

Other information relating to the year ending 31 March 2018:

- A further 500,000 shares were issued paid up to $1 per share on 1 September 2017.
- The land was revalued up by $100,000.
- The net profit before tax was $890,436. The income tax rate is 28%.
- The directors had declared a final dividend of $5,000 for the year ended 31 March 2017 and this was paid on 15 June 2017.
- The company paid an interim dividend of 1.5 cents per share to all shareholders on 30 September 2017.
- The directors declared on 10 August 2017, a final dividend of $6,000 for the year ended 31 March 2018.

Required:
- Prepare the worksheet to calculate the changes in equity for the business.
- Statement of Changes in Equity for the year ended 31 March 2018.
- Prepare the Shareholders' Funds section of the Balance Sheet as at 31 March 2018.

Solution ~ Washdyke Tilers Limited

	Capital	Retained Earnings	ARR	Balance
Opening Balances	1,000,000	1,035,132	150,000	2,185,132
Additional 500,000 shares @ $1 per share	500,000			500,000
Net profit after tax		641,114		641,114
Final dividend		-5,000		-5,000
Interim dividend		-15,000		-15,000
Devaluation of property				0
Revaluation of property and plant			100,000	100,000
Closing Balances	1,500,000	1,656,246	250,000	3,406,246

Washdyke Tilers Limited
Statement of Changes in Equity
for the year ending 31 March 2018

	$	$	$
Shareholders' funds at the start of the year			
Issued share capital (500,000 shares at issue price $2.00)		1,000,000	
Retained earnings		1,035,132	
Asset revaluation reserve (property and plant)		150,000	2,185,132
Additional 500,000 shares issued (September 2017) @ $1.00	500,000		
Add NPAT	641,114		
Increase in ARR	100,000	1,241,114	
Deduct dividends:			
previous year's final dividend (June 2017)	5,000		
interim dividend on all shares September 2017)	15,000	20,000	
Deduct devaluation of property			1,221,114
Shareholders' funds at the end of the year			$3,406,246

profit for year $890,436
tax at 28% $249,322
$641,114

1,000,000 shares * 1.5 cents = $15,000

Washdyke Tilers Limited
Balance Sheet
as at 31 March 2018

	$	$	$
Shareholders' Funds			
Issued capital	1,500,000		
Retained earnings	1,656,246	3,156,246	
Asset Revaluation reserve		250,000	
			$3,406,246

$150,000 plus $100,000

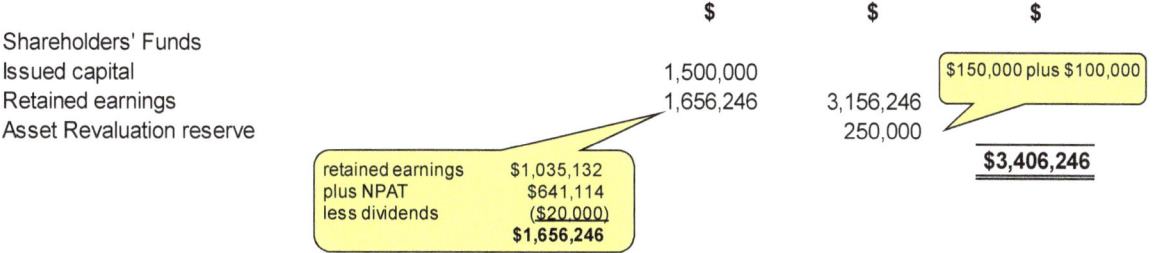

retained earnings $1,035,132
plus NPAT $641,114
less dividends ($20,000)
$1,656,246

Author Background

I am a trained teacher and have a Master's degree, diplomas in computing and belong to the Institute of Management. I have been a teacher/lecturer for the past 30 years: firstly nine years at secondary level then for the past 21 years at tertiary institutions teaching to graduate level. Over these many years I have purchased hundreds of technical texts. What I have found though is (apart from a couple of texts), I was probably only 'pulling out' one or two areas of information from each book and they have then just sat on my study shelves.

About five years ago, I finally decided there had to be a different way to approach each of my lessons. This is when I created topic booklets. Each booklet represents all that I need for a two hour teaching session: theory, worked tasks, practical tasks and solutions and a review of the lesson. Occasionally of course, dependent on the needs of the students, there might be a need to have another session on a topic – but again, I could use the same format but with additional practical tasks.

These topic booklets are my teaching plan/my guide – but of course it is equally important on how it is presented in front of the students. If the material is there and you are comfortable with it, then you are relaxed in front of the students. Dependent upon the discipline or topic, I still use PowerPoint and other interactive resources.

It is my intention to make life easier for teachers/tutors. If there is a topic that you would like covered; I would welcome suggestions and it would be my pleasure to create a topic book for you (so long as it was within my expertise of course).

Quite importantly, if you find errors in my work; or do not understand my rationale behind a concept – I would be most grateful if you drew that to my attention. Note: For introductory concept teaching in this discipline, I have omitted sales tax (VAT or GST); as I feel there is sufficient learning with new concepts before introducing the 'applied' aspects.

I have taken great care not to infringe on other people's work; although it is hard not to pick up ideas and to develop from those ideas. Likewise, there is so much generic material that I have found repeated in a number of different publications. The amount of help that in recent years is made available on the Internet is a credit to the generosity of the people who provide it (both written ideas, tutorials, YouTube) and again, I have gained knowledge from these sources. However, if anyone feels that my theory or task storylines are too similar to their own – then please let me know and I will alter my material accordingly. I have purchased my own graphics software (IMSI) but occasionally also use free graphics from Google. Any drawings or cartoon strips are my own.

What I have found is that a self-contained lesson topic is what is needed – and that is why and how I have developed my 'lesson plans'.

I hope that you find these topic books helpful.

Contact Details:

Judith Pope
teachatopic@gmail.com

© J Pope 2018